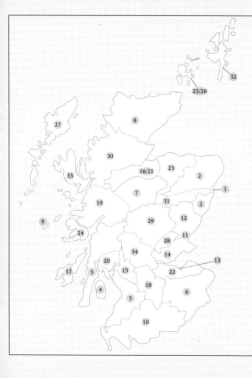

1. Aberd...
2. Aberd...
3. Argyll...
4. The I...
5. Arran...
6. The I...
7. The C...
8. Caithness & Sutherland
9. Coll & Tiree
10. Dumfries & Galloway
11. Dundee
12. Dundee & Angus
13. Edinburgh
14. Fife, Kinross & Clackmannan
15. Glasgow
16. Inverness
17. Islay, Jura, Colonsay & Oronsay

26. Orkney in Wartime
27. The Outer Hebrides
28. The City of Perth
29. Highland Perthshire
30. Ross & Cromarty
31. Royal Deeside
32. Shetland
33. The Isle of Skye
34. Stirling & The Trossachs

The remaining six books, *Caledonia*, *Distinguished Distilleries*, *Sacred Scotland*, *Scotland's Mountains*, *Scotland's Wildlife* and *The West Highland Way* feature locations in various parts of the country, so are not included in the map list above.

PICTURING SCOTLAND

COLL & TIREE

COLIN & EITHNE NUTT
Authors and photographers

2 Tiree has become Scotland's wind-surfing and kite-surfing 'capital', due to the combination of these characteristics – a long sandy bay and plenty of wind. On days when conditions are ideal, the sky

COLL & TIREE

...can be full of kites as pictured, giving the surfers an exhilarating ride along the waves.

Welcome to Coll & Tiree!

Between the Isles of Coll and Tiree and Canada stretches nothing, other than the vast Atlantic Ocean. Low-lying as these islands are, they are subject to all that the Atlantic throws at them in times of storm and tempest, for they are the first landfall for the prevailing winds and currents that sweep across that mighty ocean. From the northern tip of Tiree, the southern end of Coll looks amazingly close. They are of similar size and while not exactly small as Scottish islands go, they are definitely 'drops in the ocean', as the picture opposite seeks to show. Lying way out to sea beyond the larger Isle of Mull, they are equally remote from the mainland, as far west as the Outer Hebrides. They look vulnerable to the forces that the surrounding elements can throw at them, lodged as they are on the faint horizon between ocean swell and unending sky. Both are accessible by ferry or by air; neither has any street lights!

However, they are most definitely not 'two peas in a pod'! Their characters are surprisingly different, so visiting both in one trip is a joy. Coll is approximately 13 miles long, three miles at its widest and has a population of around 200 all-year residents. A herd of Hebridean sheep is nurtured there as is a herd of rare Eriskay ponies along with other livestock. There are masses of birds and an abundance of flora and fauna. Unlike Tiree, Coll has some trees and a more

From the sea, Tiree looks vulnerable to the forces of nature. Mostly low-lying, it is sometimes 5
referred to either as 'the land below the waves', or a raised beach.

up-hill-down-dale topography. It has many hidden, glorious beaches and places of historical interest. Its excellent hotel comes complete with helipad! A café and interesting shops are located in the village of Arinagour where most people live.

Tiree, on the other hand, is 12 miles long, six miles at its widest point and devoid of woodland and has a population of around 770. Its villages are spread throughout the island. Sea and sky simply stretch out. It has three sizeable hills but otherwise the landscape is flat – nothing to spoil the view, so to speak! There are vast expanses of white sandy beaches and multitudes of birds and other wildlife. Tiree is one of the sunniest places in Britain, blessed as it is by the Gulf Stream which makes winter temperatures generally higher than on the mainland. But there it is also wind, wind and more wind: of great advantage to those who employ its force to enjoy water sports of many varieties while one of the spinoff benefits is that midges are almost non-existent in summer!

6   An impressive whalebone arch stands above the pier at Arinagour, welcoming visitors to Coll as they arrive on the ferry.

Both islands suffered from the 'Clearances' in earlier centuries, which occurred when landowners decided to move the islanders from their crofts for their own monetary gain. Many headed for Canada, Australia and America, leaving behind their roots, their family and their ruined crofts, many of which still bear testament to those dreadful times.

These islands abound with rare species of birds such as the corncrake, which elsewhere is in decline and lapwings, which have also decreased in number since the 19th century. There are many species of orchid, some particular to the island environment but all with their own outstanding beauty. Walking or cycling are both very good ways in which to explore the islands with the opportunity to be able to *listen* as well as to see: the sound of the wind, the sound of the waves, birdsong, the lowing of cattle, sheep and lambs and the occasional pony. Then, when night falls and the sky grows dark, the stars all come out to play . . .

The Isle of Tiree is a relative stronghold for the rare, elusive corncrake – far more often heard than seen! A summer visitor, its numbers appear to be in decline.

8   Arinagour (meaning 'goat point') is the only village on Coll and is where about half of the island's
    population lives. This evening view looks south across the harbour. The bay along which Arinagour

...s situated is named Loch Eatharna. Being on the south side of the island, it provides a relatively ...sheltered anchorage.

10 This is the opposite view to the one on the previous pages, looking towards the head of the bay with the white-painted Coll Hotel visible near the centre, just below the skyline.

Left: heron in Arinagour; above right: An Cridhe (meaning 'the heart') – the Isle of Coll's new **11** community centre; below right: a carved panel in An Cridhe depicting part of Arinagour.

12 A tranquil evening scene in Arinagour. The Coll Parish Church is silhouetted on the skyline;
the Coll Hotel's lights are reflected in the bay.

While a dark night-time sky is considered a normal aspect of life on Coll, three locations are allocated specifically for Dark Sky viewing, including Arinagour, where this image was taken.

14 These lovely, rare Eriskay ponies are kept in fields just north of Arinagour.

The road north of Arinagour is in places lined with an ancient-looking stone wall that looks rather like a row of standing stones. Now supplemented by a fence, it remains a pleasing feature.

16 Up in the East End of Coll, some fascinating geology in the form of these reddish rocks, contorted by the huge forces exerted upon them into swirling strata of varied hues.

The rocks opposite are to be found on the coast near Cornaig, where this rocky bay provides a picture-perfect location for a spot of rock pool exploration – or just a place to stand and stare.

18 A flock of Hebridean sheep bred on Coll. They are renowned for their excellent wool. They rushed to meet us and posed beautifully!

Traditional crofting cottages remain in use, and well-kept examples add a welcome splash of colour
to the landscape. The bathtub is presumably no longer used for its original purpose . . .

20 At the northern tip of Coll is Sorisdale's deserted village. On stormy days, locations like this are sombre in mood, evocative perhaps of the circumstances that brought about their desertion . . .

. . . whereas on a brighter day, the ruins take on a picturesque charm. Despite the likely privations, **21** life here in the past clearly had its compensations.

22 Elsewhere in the village, nature is reclaiming the land, with the remains of this building providing a wind-break for these stunted trees.

But some of the old buildings remain broadly intact, with these two demonstrating different roofing **23** styles of turf (left) and thatch. Inset: pockets of wild primroses grow along road verges.

24 A quick flit now to the other end of Coll (the West End) where, from the top of huge sand dunes, a panoramic view of the Breachacha Estate reveals the 'new' Breachacha Castle of 1750 on the

left, the original 15th-century castle, centre, and the farm steading on the right, where substantial 25
renovation and redevelopment is underway.

26 Returning to Coll's north coast at Cliad Bay, large numbers of seals can often be seen basking on the skerries. These are Harbour, a.k.a. Common, seals. Seals you might expect to see . . .

. . . but alpacas?? Continuing down Coll's north coast road, a species definitely not native to **27** Scotland may be found: these alpacas enjoy island life. They produce wonderful, soft wool.

28 The highest point on Coll is Ben Hogh, (104m/341ft), near the summit of which is this precariously perched rock, named Clach na Ban Righ (the Queen's Stone).

The view from Ben Hogh is superb, this south-westerly aspect showing Loch Ballyhaugh **29** at lower right, the Hebridean Centre next to it and wonderful Hogh Bay beyond.

30 And down at Hogh Bay, this ewe and her lamb seem to be enjoying their 'patch'. It's the day after a storm and big waves are still rolling onto the beach.

A flock of oystercatchers are spooked by something (perhaps one of the larger gulls or a skua)
and suddenly take flight, adding their striking black and white profiles to the scene.

32 Those big breakers are hitting the rocky outcrops at the north end of the bay with impressive force, giving onlookers the splendid sight of this watery explosion.

Crannogs on Loch Cliad: the stone wall points to the remains of an ancient dwelling on this islet. **33**
Further right, the smaller islet may be man-made, to serve the same purpose. Taking these pictures can

34 bring unexpected hazards: one minute these cattle (bull included!) were the other side of the fence; the next they had walked around the end of it and were eyeing the photographer at close quarters.

Inland from Hogh Bay, these two standing stones are at Totronald. They are called Na Sgeulachan **35** in Gaelic ('teller of tales' in English) and may have been used for astronomical purposes.

36 Now a closer look at Breachacha Castle (first seen on p.24/5). It was thought to have been the seat of the MacLeans of Mull. Although restored, it remains a good example of a medieval fortress.

The massive sand dunes at Coll's West End provide an excellent vantage point. With an eroded **37** patch of dune in the foreground, beyond is the rocky outline of Ben Feall.

38 The road doesn't reach the extremity of the West End, but walking (or cycling) the couple of miles around Crossapol Bay to this old cemetery provides a rewarding seaward view.

Now it's time to bid Coll farewell and set sail for Tiree. The voyage of an hour or so presents a continuous panoramic profile of Coll, then Tiree. Look out for dolphins!

40 As noted in the introduction, Tiree and Coll get the full force of the Atlantic Ocean, particularly on their north-west facing coasts. Big seas can persist for a few days after a storm, enabling the sight of

huge breakers like these crashing onto the shore, as seen here at Balevuillin.

42 Arriving at Tiree: from the ferry, this is the island's principal village of Scarinish where its houses are dotted around – all the more charming for its informal arrangement.

Various members of Calmac's fleet serve Coll and Tiree. Here, *Lord of the Isles* ('Loti' to her friends), **43** leans in the swell as she turns to manoeuvre up to the pier at Scarinish.

44 The fishing boat *Strenuous* returns to Scarinish harbour, bathed in evening light. Our tour of Tiree will be a clockwise circuit of the island, beginning in Scarinish and ending at Gott Bay.

Scarinish sunrise: not quite risen yet, but already under-lighting the clouds to beautiful effect. **45**
The cottage on the right is typical of many on Tiree.

46 About 20 minutes later, the warming glow of those early, near-horizontal rays are giving the village a gentle wake-up call. Another fine day is in prospect.

Switching back to evening light combined with low tide, and the outline of a vessel from yesteryear   **47**
still casts shadows from the spiky remnants of its structure.

48 Tiree is a fertile island – its name means 'land of corn'. Here, Island House stands on what was once an island in the appropriately named Loch an Eilean. Inset: lapwings are plentiful on Tiree.

Tiree is home to a rich variety of wild flowers. Three of Tiree's orchids are, left: Common Spotted
orchid; centre: Early Marsh orchid – a local variety; right: Pyramidal orchid.

50 The cairn in memory of Revd Donald MacCallum, minister of Heylipol in the 1880s, stands in a field at Kilkenneth. The inquisitive cows could not have arranged themselves more photogenically

if the photographer had been able to position them himself! The church that stands near Heylipol today is the 1906-built Tiree Parish Church.

52 While heading for the south of Tiree, a brief stop at the southern end of Crossapol Bay captures this moody moment of rainfall out at sea and sunshine on the shore.

Hynish is Tiree's most southerly settlement where this tidy and well-kept farm provides an aesthetically pleasing scene of agricultural efficiency. Inset: a pair of Greylag geese pose tidily too!

54 These buildings in Hynish were started in 1837 and comprised a dock, workshops and lodgings for those involved in the building of Skerryvore Lighthouse. On the right is the Signal Tower,

built to communicate with the lighthouse, 10.5 miles out to sea. Above is the dock where the **55** 4,300+ stone blocks needed for the lighthouse were loaded into the vessels that took them to the site.

56 The highest point on Tiree at 141m/462ft is Carnan Mor (locally known as Ben Hynish), the hill on which the 'Golfball' radar station (see p.42) is located. The north-easterly view from here extends

the length of Tiree, with Scarinish visible on the land in the lower half of the picture. Coll lies beyond, with Ardnamurchan on the mainland in the far distance.

58 The northerly view from Ben Hynish gives a good idea of much of Tiree's landscape, with Loch a' Phuill prominent in the centre. Beinn Hough breaks the horizon at top left.

To the west, the settlement of Balephuil overlooks the bay of the same name. The cover picture **59** shows the full extent of this bay, through to Ceann a' Mhara – see also p.62.

60 Down on Traigh Bhi, the beach that lines Balephuil Bay, one of the gentler forms of water sport – paddle boarding – is enjoyed on a day of calm and sparkly sea.

Loch a' Phuill is drained by the Abhainn a' Bheidhe, which is pictured here as it crosses Traigh Bhi. **61**
Balephuil village can be seen in the distance on the slopes of Ben Hynish.

62 From the slopes of Beinn Hough, to the south lie Kilkenneth and Sandaig, with the craggy hill of Ceann a' Mhara rising beyond. This is the other side of the hill in the cover picture.

And looking east from Beinn Hough, more of Tiree's neat farmlands, Loch Bhasapoll at upper right **63** and Balephetrish Bay in the distance. Coll is on the horizon.

64 Several examples of traditional 'black houses' remain in use around Tiree. The upper picture shows one in the setting of the spread-out village of Balevuillin; the lower one is nearby.

Down in Balevuillin Bay, the sea may be having a rough day, but these two seabirds seemingly **65** remain unruffled. On the left is an oystercatcher; its little friend is a turnstone.

66 Tiree does not get snow that often, but here it is in the depths of winter. It's interesting to see how the addition of snow throws the fence posts into such sharp relief – try counting them!

Moving east around the north of Tiree, this is Cornaig water mill. It is slowly but surely being **67** restored and the water wheel is in working order.

68 The long shore line of Balephetrish Bay is worth exploring to seek out the rock arches like this one, with its array of brightly coloured and sea-smoothed stone.

The 'architecture' produced by millions of years of coastal erosion creates shapes and colour **69** schemes that are different at every turn. Add in some rock pooling and the day just goes by . . .

70 . . . until the sun goes down amid some extraordinary cloud shapes and the contrasting light effects grip the gaze.

A walk east from Balephetrish leads to the Ringing Stone, so named because of the metallic ring it **71** emits when struck. It also has several 'cup' markings, probably made in Neolithic times.

72 Further east along the coast at Vaul is Dun Mor broch, the best example of this type of structure on Tiree. Built about 60AD as an emergency refuge, it was then inhabited for 200-300 years.

Close by Dun Mor, the flat-topped hillock in the centre of the picture was also an inhabited 'dun' or fort. On close inspection, some evidence of structures can be made out.

74 Sea Thrift thrives around Tiree's coast, favouring rocky outcrops and providing a welcome splash of pink in spring and early summer.

Trees are few on Tiree. This variety is the most common, often found by a windbreak of some form, **75** such as that provided by this house in Milton at the northern tip of Tiree.

76 We come full circle when arriving at Gott Bay, the longest on the island, which makes it ideal for wind-surfing and kite-surfing. This kite is just getting airborne.

These two kite-surfers are achieving a good turn of speed. When the wind direction is just right, **77** the kites can be turned 180 degrees . . .

78 . . . which can lift the surfer well out of the water. Centre and right: wind-surfing continues to be the preferred option for many.

And so with one last look back around the broad sweep of Gott Bay, it's time to board the ferry home.
Farewell to Tiree . . . and Coll . . . until the next time.

Published 2019 by Lyrical Scotland, an imprint of Lomond Books Ltd, Broxburn, EH52 5NF
www.lyricalscotland.com www.lomondbooks.com

Originated by Ness Publishing, 47 Academy Street, Elgin, Moray, IV30 1LR

Printed in China

All photographs © Colin and Eithne Nutt except pp.7, 49 & 66 © Anne M Stanley

Text © Colin & Eithne Nutt
ISBN 978-1-78818-080-1

Front cover: Balephuil Bay from Ben Hynish; p.1: twin lambs at Arinagour; p.4: a courteous welcome to Coll;
this page: wartime gun near Arinagour pier; back cover: evening sky over Balephetrish Bay, Tiree